GOD'S HOLY DARKNESS

SHAREI GREEN AND BECKAH SELNICK

ILLUSTRATED BY NIKKI FAISON

beaming
books

MINNEAPOLIS

Darkness and **blackness** and **night**

are too often compared

to **lightness** and **whiteness** and **day**

and found deficient,

but let us **name** the **beauty**

and **goodness**

and **holiness**

of **darkness** and **blackness** and **night**.

God uses darkness and blackness and
night to show love for the world.

Creation began in the dark.

"In the beginning … darkness covered the face of the deep"
(Genesis 1:1–2).

God poured out love and brought all things into being.

Creation is God's work done in holy darkness.

When Abraham began to doubt God's promises,

the Lord took him on a walk and pointed to the night sky.

"Look toward the heaven and count the stars, if you are able to count them . . .
so shall your descendants be"

(Genesis 15:5).

Later, Jacob wrestled all night with God and was changed forever.

The beginning of the many nations and peoples of the Lord

is the work of God's beautiful darkness.

At midnight,

the Lord passed over Egypt

and set the people free.

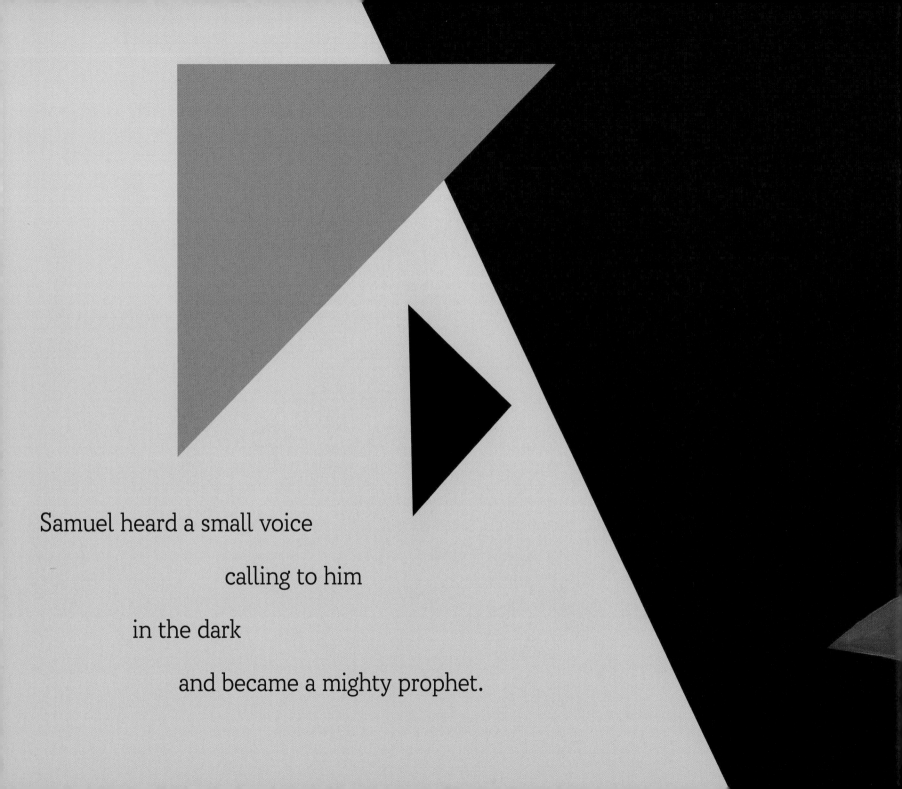

Samuel heard a small voice

calling to him

in the dark

and became a mighty prophet.

The LORD Appears to Samuel

3 In those days, when the boy Samuel was serving the LORD under the direction of Eli, there were very few messages from the LORD, and visions from him were quite rare. 2One night Eli, who was now almost blind, was sleeping in his own room; 3Samuel was sleeping in the sanctuary, where the sacred Covenant Box was. Before dawn, while the lamp was still burning, 4the LORD called Samuel. He answered, "Yes, sir!" 5and ran to Eli and said, "You called me, and here I am."

But Eli answered, "I didn't call you; go back to bed." So Samuel went back to bed.

6The LORD called Samuel again. The boy did not know that it was the LORD, because the LORD had never spoken to him before. So he got up, went to Eli, and said, "You called me, and here I am."

But Eli answered, "My son, I didn't call you; go back to bed."

8The LORD called Samuel a third time; he got up, went to Eli, and said, "You called me, and here I am."

Then Eli realized that it was the LORD who was calling the boy, 9so he said to him, "Go back to bed; and if he calls you again, say, 'Speak, LORD, your servant is listening.'" So Samuel went back to bed.

10The LORD came and stood there, and called as he had before, "Samuel! Samuel!"

Samuel answered, "Speak; your servant is listening."

11The LORD said to him, "Some day I am going to do something to the people of Israel that is so terrible that everyone who hears about it will be stunned. 12On that day I will carry out all my threats against Eli's family, from beginning to end. 13I have already

told him that I am going to punish his family forever because his sons have spoken against me. Eli knew they were doing this, but he did not stop them. 14So I solemnly declare to the family of Eli that no sacrifice or offering will ever be able to remove the consequences of this terrible sin."

15Samuel stayed in bed until morning, then got up and opened the doors of the house of the LORD. He was afraid to tell Eli about the vision. 16Eli called him, "Samuel, my boy!"

"Yes, sir," answered Samuel.

17"What did the LORD tell you?" Eli asked. "Don't keep anything from me. God will punish you severely if you don't tell me everything he said."

18So Samuel told him everything; he did not keep anything back. Eli said, "He is the LORD; he will do what he thinks best."

19As Samuel grew up, the LORD was with him and made come true everything that Samuel said. 20So all the people of Israel, from one end of the country to the other, knew that Samuel was indeed a prophet of the LORD. 21The LORD continued to reveal himself at Shiloh, where he had first revealed himself to Samuel through his word. And when Samuel spoke, all Israel listened.

When the temple was complete,

King Solomon said,

"The Lord has said he would dwell in thick darkness"

(1 Kings 8:12).

The spirit of God dwells in the holy darkness where

we are invited to be held in God's love.

Angels

appeared to the shepherds

in the dark

and told them of a baby in a manger.

The disciples gathered with Jesus for the Holy Supper

as the day

turned

to night.

When Jesus died on the cross,

the day went black from noon to three.

Creation began in holy darkness,

    and our new lives as free people in Christ began

in the darkness of the sky that day.

God saved all creation,

and it was the work of God's beautiful,

                        good,

                          and holy darkness.

Rich, black soil

brings forth

abundant life.

"Unless a grain of wheat falls
into the earth and dies, it remains
just a single grain, but if it dies,
it bears much fruit"

(John 12:24).

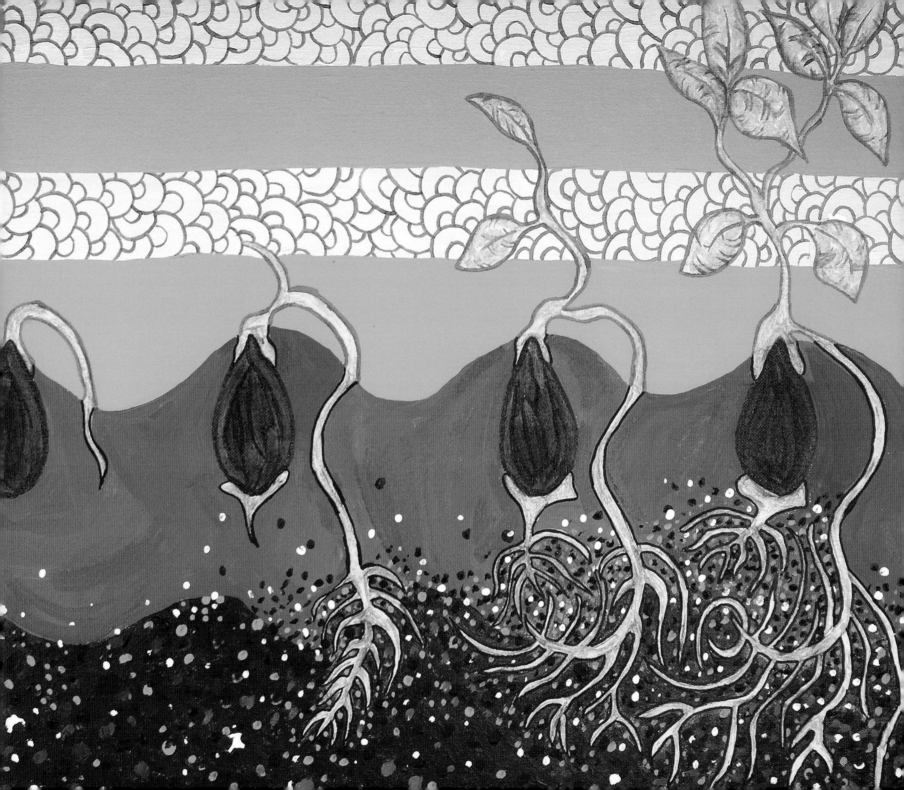

The deep dark of the ocean

holds more life

than has even been discovered.

We are reminded of the size

of God's creation through

the boundless beautiful black

of outer space.

From the beginning of creation to the stars in the night sky,

we are shown God's love.

In houses of worship with dark spaces for wonder,

we are held in God's love.

In the dark soil and the deep sea,

we are reminded of God's love.

From the promise of peace made to the

shepherds at night

to the promise Jesus made on the cross,

these are the beautiful works

of **God's holy darkness**.

A Note for Caregivers

IN OUR WORLD AND IN OUR LIVES, Blackness should be celebrated. Darkness should foster wonder and awe. And we should find comfort and rest in the night. But instead, we usher in light/dark binaries. Look to John 1:5: "The light shall shine in the darkness and the darkness shall not overcome it." This passage speaks of literal lightness and darkness, but we have ascribed qualities of "good" versus "bad" to light and darkness, with light being "good" and dark being "bad." With the construct of race, these attributes were given to people with light-colored skin (white) and people with dark-colored skin (Black and brown). But we are called, and always have been called, to disrupt this binary thinking and, ultimately, disrupt and dismantle the systems that value lightness over darkness, whiteness over Blackness.

God's Holy Darkness features beloved Bible stories. Sometimes, we know stories so well, we forget to listen to them. This book challenges us to hear those stories in a new way. To hear the stories of the beauty and holiness and goodness of Blackness and darkness and night. Read these words and ask questions. What other ways can we challenge our perceptions of race in church and theology? When you imagine God, Jesus, or other biblical figures, what do they look like? What images have you seen? What images are hung in your church buildings? Look, and listen, at what is there. Look, and listen, for what is missing. Seek comfort and rest at night, wonder at the mystery of the dark, celebrate Blackness. Disrupt the binary and welcome *God's Holy Darkness.*

About the authors and illustrator

SHAREI GREEN is pursuing a master of divinity as a seminarian at the Lutheran School of Theology at Chicago. Sharei has a strong commitment to community healing and sabbath, especially in BIPOC communities. You can find her writings online at *Living Lutheran*, *Gather Magazine*, and *Café Magazine*.

BECKAH SELNICK is a writer focusing on storytelling for digital formats. She is the host and creator of *PK/PK Podcast*. Beckah is living at the intersection of faith, funny, and feminism in Portland, Oregon.

NIKKI FAISON is a pastor in the Evangelical Lutheran Church in America serving as the program director for African Descent Ministries. Nikki is the creator of *MONadvocacy*, a racial justice resource grounded in play. She is passionate about queer Black liberation, cultivating diverse leadership in faith spaces, and the art of creation. She resides in the Chicagoland area with her spouse, daughter, and two cats, Penne Pablo and Rigatoni Braxton.

Published in 2022 by Beaming Books, an imprint of 1517 Media. All rights reserved. No part of this book may be reproduced without the written permission of the publisher. Email copyright@1517.media. Printed in the United States of America.

28 27 26 25 24 23 22   1 2 3 4 5 6 7 8

Hardcover ISBN: 978-1-5064-8241-5
Ebook ISBN: 978-1-5064-8345-0

Library of Congress Cataloguing-in-Publication Data
Names: Green, Sharei, author. | Selnick, Beckah, author. | Nikki Faison, illustrator.
Title: God's holy darkness / by Sharei Green and Beckah Selnick; illustrated by Nikki Faison.
Description: Minneapolis, MN : Beaming Books, 2022. | Audience: Ages 5-8 |
Summary: "In God's Holy Darkness, Sharei Green and Beckah Selnick deconstruct anti-Blackness in Christian theology by celebrating instances in the story of God's people when darkness, blackness, and night are beautiful, good, and holy. Perfect for reading and anti-racist reflection in worship, as an affirmation and celebration with children, and at home with caregivers, God's Holy Darkness is a gift to cherish" – Provided by publisher.
Identifiers: LCCN 2021058103 (print) | LCCN 2021058104 (ebook) | ISBN 9781506482415 (hardcover) | ISBN 9781506483450 (ebook)
Subjects: LCSH: Light and darkness in the Bible–Juvenile literature. | Black–Religious aspects–Christianity–Juvenile literature.
Classification: LCC BS680.L53 G74 2022 (print) | LCC BS680.L53 (ebook) |
DDC 220.95–dc23/eng/20220121
LC record available at https://lccn.loc.gov/2021058103
LC ebook record available at https://lccn.loc.gov/2021058104

VN0004589; 9781506482415; MAY2022

Beaming Books
PO Box 1209
Minneapolis, MN 55440-1209